KNOW GOD,
NO FEAR

Stephen Elkins

Narrated by Joni Eareckson Tada

Illustrations by Jesse Reisch

Broadman & Holman Publishers   Nashville, Tennessee

The LORD is my light and my salvation—whom shall I fear?

PSALM 27:1

The old church van rattled and shook as it bounced down the old country road. The sound of kids singing poured from the open windows, reaching the ears of some very curious forest critters.

"How much longer 'til we get there?" Bobby asked. "How about now!" said Miss Johnson as they passed an old wooden sign that read, "Campsite 1 Mile." Soon the excited campers and their two brave leaders hurried out of the van.

"Everyone get your gear ready," instructed Mrs. Bailey.
"It will be dark in an hour, so let's not waste any time."
In minutes they were on the trail to the campsite.
Step-by-step the hikers journeyed down the narrow
pathway. They were still singing, excited about
spending their first night under the stars!

Soon the narrow pathway opened into a beautiful
campsite. "OK, everybody! Let's set up our tents and
get ready to roast some marshmallows!" As the tents
went up, Miss Johnson went to work gathering wood
for the campfire. Suddenly, in the midst of all the
unpacking, there came an unfamiliar "thump, thump"
and a thrashing of leaves.

"What was that?" asked Bobby. As Miss Johnson was bringing an armload of firewood, the kids came running towards her, nearly knocking her down.   Seeing the frightened looks on their faces she asked, "What's wrong? Is everything alright?"

"We heard a sound in the woods. Something's out there!" they exclaimed. "Something big."

"Now, kids, we're in the forest now. It was probably a couple of squirrels chasing each other through the leaves," Mrs. Bailey explained calmly.   She paused for a moment and then said, "Do you know what my mother used to say when I was frightened? She'd say, if you know God, there's no fear!"

"Know God, no fear...what does that mean?" asked Sally.

"It means the more we know about God, the less we'll be afraid. Then my mother would tell me the story of David the shepherd boy," Mrs. Bailey explained.

"We know about David," said Jake. "He fought the giant Goliath. He wasn't afraid of anything."

"Well, actually, David had many fears and he wrote about them in the Book of Psalms. David said, 'When I am afraid, I will trust in God.' I'm sure each one of us has been afraid sometime and it's good to share your fear with others. But it's even better to share them with God."

Then came a hesitant voice, "Mrs. Bailey, can I share one of
my fears?" asked Matt. "My biggest fear is being alone.
I always feel safer when someone is with me."

Mrs. Bailey spoke again, "Can you imagine
being out here all alone?"

"Oh, no," they all said.

"Well, David spent many nights all alone tending his sheep.
But he knew God was with him. He wrote, 'The Lord is
with me and comforts me.' If you feel frightened because
you're alone, know that God is with you.
Remember, know God, no fear."

Miss Johnson got the fire blazing as the kids continued to talk about their fears. "I get anxious not knowing what's going to happen tomorrow," said Caroline. "Who knows what could happen to me or my family?"

"God knows everything that's going to happen," said Miss Johnson. "Imagine, David waking up each morning looking for green pastures. He never knew what the day would bring. But David had a verse that calmed his fear of tomorrow. 'My times are in your hands,' he wrote. He knew God would take care of tomorrow."

"Know God, no fear!" the kids said with a smile.

"Now you're getting it," said Mrs. Bailey.

Then, Kevin who rarely spoke chimed in, "My biggest fear is speaking in front of people and making new friends. Did David have a verse for me?"

"It was very brave of you to share that with us, Kevin. David knew that fear can keep us from making new friends, and he does have a verse for you, 'The Lord is my strength. Whom shall I fear?' Did you know that David had a best friend named Jonathan. Jonathan's father was King Saul. Jonathan even saved David's life. What if David had been afraid of meeting new people? They may never have become friends. Remember, the Lord is your strength. Know God..." began Mrs. Bailey.

"No fear!" came the confident response from the kids.

Ron hesitated, then spoke, "Mrs. Bailey, sometimes I'm afraid of the dark. I'm sure David the giant killer was never afraid of the dark, was he?"

"I'm sure David had some scary moments in the dark just like we do. But he wrote in Psalm 27 'The Lord is my light and my salvation. In whom shall I fear.' We can have that kind of confidence too, even in the dark. Just know God..." led Mrs. Bailey. "No fear!" came the resounding response.

Suddenly, there came another "thump, thump" and the thrashing of leaves...closer and louder this time. Before Miss Johnson could speak, Sally blurted out, "Sometimes I hear noises at night. Strange noises. I imagine there's a monster in my room and I get so afraid."

"Our imagination can turn tiny noises into giant fears. I imagine David heard noises at night too. But he had a verse that was just perfect. He wrote, 'The Lord delivers me from all my fears,' even the ones we imagine. Once again, if we know God, He helps calm the fear."

"But what about bad things that happen? When buildings fall and tornadoes blow houses away? Aren't we supposed to be afraid of that?" asked Ted.

"Certainly, we should use caution and do what our parents and teachers ask when a storm is approaching. But being careful is not the same thing as being afraid. When David faced a storm he said he would not fear even though the mountains shake and the waters rage. How could he be so brave?"

"He knew God was with him," said Bobby. "And when we know God, we have no fear."

Suddenly one of the tents began to move. Then came that familiar "thump, thump, thump". "L-o-o-o-k! Sally's monster is in the tent!"

Then came the sound of something breaking and the most horrible crunching sounds they'd ever heard. "It's a monster!" shouted Kevin. "Listen to those teeth."

"Children, stand back." But before Mrs. Bailey could finish her statement, out of the tent came two furry little critters covered with egg shells and pancake flour. As they disappeared into the forest, Mrs. Bailey finished her sentence with a sigh, "Know God..."

"No fear!" the kids giggled.

As the excitement ended, Miss Johnson reflected. "Two little raccoons became a monster in our imaginations. Kids, from now on let's always remember, Know God..." she paused. "No fear!" came their response.

When all the kids were finally in their tents, Mrs. Bailey turned out her lamp. The flames from the campfire created just enough light to see that all was well. "No fear?" asked Mrs. Bailey. "Know God, no fear," came a sleepy chorus.

"Who, who-o-o-o-o?" said the night owl.

Bobby replied, "God, that's who."

And all was well under God's starry sky.